Horned Lizards

by Cari Meister

Bullfrog Books

Ideas for Parents and Teachers

Bullfrog Books let children practice reading informational text at the earliest reading levels. Repetition, familiar words, and photo labels support early readers.

Before Reading

- Discuss the cover photo. What does it tell them?

- Look at the picture glossary together. Read and discuss the words.

Read the Book

- "Walk" through the book and look at the photos. Let the child ask questions. Point out the photo labels.

- Read the book to the child, or have him or her read independently.

After Reading

- Prompt the child to think more. Ask: Have you seen a horned lizard? What other animals have horns?

Bullfrog Books are published by Jump!
5357 Penn Avenue South
Minneapolis, MN 55419
www.jumplibrary.com

Library of Congress Cataloging-in-Publication Data

Meister, Cari, author.
  Horned lizards / by Cari Meister.
    Pages cm. — (Bullfrog books. Reptile world)
  Summary: "This photo-illustrated book for beginning readers describes the physical features and behaviors of horned lizards. Includes picture glossary and index."—Provided by publisher.
  Audience: Ages 5–8.
  Audience: K to grade 3.
  Includes index.
  ISBN 978-1-62031-196-7 (hardcover: alk. paper) — ISBN 978-1-62496-283-7 (ebook)
1. Horned toads—Juvenile literature.
2. Texas horned lizard—Juvenile literature.
[1. Lizards.] I. Title.
QL666.L267.M45 2016
597.95—dc23

2014042730

Editor: Jenny Fretland VanVoorst
Series Designer: Ellen Huber
Book Designer: Michelle Sonnek
Photo Researcher: Michelle Sonnek

Photo Credits: Animals Animals, 20–21; ardea, 20–21; Corbis, cover, 1, 8–9, 12–13, 23bl; Dreamstime, 4; iStock, 6–7; National Geographic, 22; Nature Picture Library, 3, 10–11, 23tl; Science Source Images, 16–17, 23br; Shutterstock, 6, 14, 15, 19; SuperStock, 24; Thinkstock, 5, 18, 23tr.

Printed in the United States of America at Corporate Graphics in North Mankato, Minnesota.

Table of Contents

Cool Tricks

A horned lizard is hungry.

He likes ants.

He waits.

Here come some ants!

Zap!

His tongue comes out.

It is sticky.

It grabs the ants.

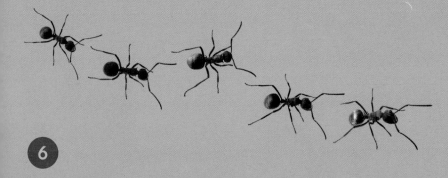

tongue

Many animals eat
horned lizards.

How do they stay safe?

They blend in with
the ground.

They are hard to see.

horns

They have a crown of horns.

It is spiky.

It is hard for animals to bite.

Oh no!

Here is a snake.

14

What will the lizard do?

He puffs up.

Now he is double his size.

He is hard to eat.

The snake goes away.

Oh no!

Here is a coyote.

What will the lizard do?

19

He shoots blood
out of his eyes!

It stings the coyote.

He runs away.

The lizard is safe.

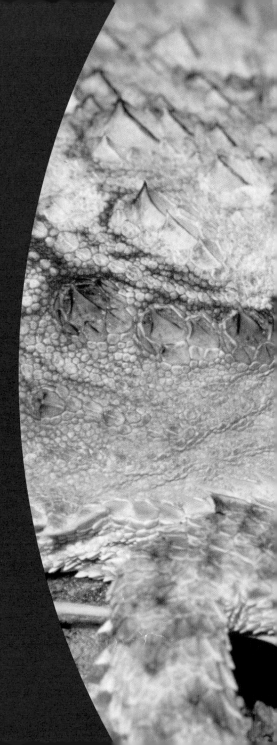

Parts of a Horned Lizard

eye
In some kinds of horned lizards, a special duct on the side of their eye can squirt blood.

skin
Sharp spines on their skin help protect the horned lizard.

toes
Horned lizards have sharp claws on their toes that are good for digging.

Picture Glossary

blend in
When an animal's skin or fur looks like the dirt and plants, making them hard to see.

coyote
A wild mammal related to the dog.

crown of horns
A bunch of poky spikes that form a circle on a lizard's head.

double
Two times the size.

Index

To Learn More

Learning more is as easy as 1, 2, 3.

1) Go to www.factsurfer.com

2) Enter "hornedlizards" into the search box.

3) Click the "Surf" button to see a list of websites.

With factsurfer.com, finding more information is just a click away.